1

Flatbread Expedition

from Marrakesh to Mumbai

50 irresistible recipes from 18 countries

Eva Seyberth

Imprint

Bibliographic information from the German National Library: The German National Library lists this publication in the German National Bibliography; detailed bibliographic data is available online at dnb.dnb.de.

Front cover photo:
Uzbek Lepeschka, photo: Eva Seyberth
Cover design:
Jacqueline Wiehl
www.webdesign-firebird.de
info@webdesign-firebird.de
1st edition 2023 (german)
2nd edition 2024 (german)

ISBN: 9798293274062

Independently published

Inhalt

Preface

Dear Readers,

Welcome to our Flatbread Expedition Around the World from Marrakech to Mumba! This book is the result of a long-standing love for Oriental cuisine. During my numerous travel adventures, I got to know the people, the dances and also the wonderful recipes in various countries in North Africa and along the Silk Roads.

Flatbreads are much more than just side dishes – they are the centerpiece of all meals! From Moroccan Khobz to Indian Parathas, 50 irresistible recipes give you a glimpse into the diversity of Middle Eastern bread culture.

Cooking connects us, it is a universal language of love and togetherness. I would like to thank everyone who has accompanied me on this flatbread expedition – from the locals who shared their family recipes with me to the travel companions who joined me in the joy of discovery and tasting.

Now I invite you to embark on your own culinary journey of discovery. Enjoy your time in the kitchen!

Good luck and bon appetit!

Sincerely, Eva Seyberth

Bread stories and origins

Bread comes from the Orient

Around 10,000 years ago, the sedentary lifestyle of humans began and the domestication of cereals began at the same time. For a long time, researchers believed that bread must logically have originated in the same period.

But this is not the case. The history of bread began several thousand years earlier.

In Göbeli-Tekke, an 11,600-year-old archaeological site in Turkey near the Syrian border, numerous bones and the remains of meals prepared from wild wheat were found. Although this was still a culture of hunter-gatherers, more grain was eaten than meat. In fact, it is said to have been ground and eaten by the tubful.

But that is by no means all. The oldest charred remains of unleavened bread to date have been found in a Natufian settlement in Jordan. These are 14,400 years old. The Natufian period represents the transitional period between Stone Age hunter-gatherers and Neolithic sedentary farmers.

Even then, the collected grains - which were still wild grass seeds - were crushed, soaked and cooked -and the porridge was "baked" on stones in the sun. The rock-hard flatbreads kept for a long time and could be turned back into porridge with water or milk at any time. They were perfect for storing and eating on the way.

Interestingly, traces of starch have been discovered in the dental calculus of early humans who lived between 40 and 46,000 years ago in both the Iran region and what is now Belgium. Bacteria that break down starch into sugar have even been identified on the 100,000-year-old remains of a Neanderthal from what is now Serbia. Charred food remains were found on 120,000-year-old hearths in South Africa, which turned out to be cell tissue from starchy plants under a scanning electron microscope.

According to the research results, the theory of the paleo-diet advocates that our ancestors only ate meat is a cliché that has long been untenable.

It is noteworthy that the collected grains were heated (roasted), fermented and soaked. In this way, beer production was discovered at the same time as the processing of grain into bread-like products. Not only in Egypt, by the way, but also in the Alps, and that as long as 5000 years ago.

The Neolithic revolution

The discovery that the first bread is much older than the first cereal fields puts the so-called Neolithic Revolution, the establishment of sedentarization and the introduction of agriculture, in a completely new light.

Gathering grass seeds was extremely laborious and time-consuming, while the need for constantly available carbohydrates was great. Bread and grain seeds, the forerunners of today's cereals, were therefore a valuable commodity that provided survival benefits. In order to ensure availability, people began to sow soaked seeds in a targeted manner.

If you wanted to protect the place with the seeds you had collected and sown from theft and animal predation, you had to stay there and guard it. This led to settlement.

Settlement in fixed locations and the cultivation of grain fields led to the creation of permanent hearths, which developed into simple ovens over time. The oldest remains of such ovens were discovered in the Indus Valley (Harappa culture, 2800-1800 BC) and in Mesopotamia, but they were probably already in use before that.

The tandur (India) is a cone-shaped tubular kiln that spread throughout the Middle East and whose name changed slightly depending on the country. The oldest traces of a tannur or tabun (Tunisia) in the western Mediterranean were found in Doña Blanca (near Cadiz) in Spain and date back to the 8th century BC.

The invention of the clay oven made it possible to distribute the heat better and more evenly, which facilitated the development of bread as a staple food.

The dough was stuck to the inside of the hot wall of the oven and baked there. The oven could heat up to 400° degrees. When the bread was baked through, it often fell into the ash embers by itself.

Grain cultivation and oven technology boosted the chances of survival and had a direct impact on population growth. It also freed up time that no longer had to be spent collecting grass seed, but could be used to develop new technologies.

Flatbread bakers in Egypt, 2007

First bakeries

The ancient Egyptians were the pioneers when it came to setting up professional bakeries. But the Sumerians also had flatbread for lunch around this time, around 5000 BC. It only reached Europe 2000 years later.

The Egyptians discovered how to make the bread soft and airy: by letting the dough stand and ferment. Natural yeasts and lactic acid bacteria from the air multiply in the dough, release carbon dioxide and loosen it.

The dough ferments, its smell changes and it gains volume. This chemical process also gives our word "bread" its name. The term comes from the Old High German "prôt", which developed from the Germanic "brauda", meaning "fermented".

In Egypt, there were later up to 30 different types of bread made from emmer and barley. In those days, who could afford which bread indicated the social position. The harder it was, the lower the social standing, the softer the bread, the higher it was. Until the Thirty Years' War, the differences in social standing also affected the type of bread available to individuals in early "Germany". From Egypt, the art of baking bread spread to Greece and from there to the Roman Empire. In the 4th century, it reached Germania and was passed on to Lithuania and Slavonia.

The first "breads" made from dried cereal porridge were also known to have originated in Europe from the oldest pile-dwelling settlements in Switzerland: flat, round cakes made from wheat and millet that were cooked on stones in the hot ashes. Ash bread was still known in the Middle Ages. The forerunner of today's oven was a clay baking bell that was placed over the stones with the food to be baked.

Beduins bake bread in the desert 2018

The original form of bread is the – unleavened – flatbread or grain cake. It is flat because it was made without a leavening agent.

In addition to the invention of the oven, there was a second decisive improvement for the further career of bread: the discovery of the fermentation process by the wild yeasts that are found in the air when bread, grape juice or vegetables begin to ferment. It was only through these yeasts that the dough was loosened and rose during baking.

The discovery of yeast

Until almost 150 years ago, however, it was not known what constitutes yeast at all. For thousands of years, bread was baked and wine and beer brewed without the ability to use specific yeasts. They brewed and baked without knowing the actual cause of fermentation. All knowledge consisted of purely empirically gained insights: trial and error – learning by doing.

Natural processes such as putrefaction, decay and fermentation were familiar to humans through their own observations and experiences. So they made use of spontaneous fermentation: simply leaving dough or fruit juice in the air led to fermentation. However, no one could answer the how? and why?

Even after sauerkraut, fish sauce, tea, cocoa and cheese had been produced, it was not really known how the acidification actually worked.

The basis for the discovery of yeast as an organism was laid in 1680 by Antoni van Leuwenhoek, who invented the first microscope-like apparatus. With it, he succeeded in identifying "spherical structures" in the fermentation substrate. Nothing more happened for a while.

It was not until 100 years later, in 1787/1788, that Antoine Laurent Lavoisier studied the fermentation process and found out that "sugar completely breaks down into alcohol and carbon dioxide". Fermentation was therefore assumed to be an oxidation process. In 1799, the French Academy of Sciences offered a prize of a kilogram bar of gold to the scientist who would finally solve the secrets of fermentation. No one has won the prize .

Until the mid-1830s, there was still a lack of clarity. Yeast was still seen as the end product of fermentation and not as its cause. It was only between 1834 and 1837 that two German and one French scientist independently made groundbreaking new discoveries:

Charles Cagniard-Latour examined beer yeast under the microscope and discovered that yeast is capable of reproduction. Theodor Schwann proved that only unsterilized air can trigger the fermentation process in sweet fruit juices. And finally, in 1834, Friedrich T. Kützing came to the conclusion that yeast causes "winy fermentation" through its "education" and "reproduction instinct", that it is of vegetable origin and not a "so-called chemical-organic compound".

Surprisingly, these new findings did not fit into the world view of some leading chemists of the time. A dispute developed that lasted for over 20 years and culminated in a defamatory article entitled "The Unravelled Secret of Mental Fermentation" (written by Friedrich Wöhler and Justus Liebig in 1839).

It was Louis Pasteur who finally put an end to all doubts and restored Mr. Wöhler and Mr. Liebig to their rightful place. He is the author of the two sentences: "No fermentation without organisms" and "Each fermentation by a specific type of organism".

From 1857 onwards, all scientists were in no doubt that yeast was a living organism that triggers fermentation.

On November 12, 1883, Emil Christian Hansen in Copenhagen succeeded in isolating a single yeast cell and growing the first pure culture of brewing yeast from it. This discovery revolutionized the art of brewing, since until then all yeasts in all breweries in the world were a mixture of top- and bottom-fermenting yeasts and bacteria. The ready availability of brewer's yeast has not only made brewing, but also baking considerably easier.

Germany became the bread basket of the world. While the ancient Egyptians were once called "bread eaters", today it is the Germans who have earned this title: with over 3,200 different types of bread, Germany has the largest selection in the world. In 2014, UNESCO declared German bread culture a World Heritage Site.

Flatbread – the original form of bread

While the Germans outdo each other in inventing new types of bread, the opposite seems to apply in the Orient: everything should be left as it has always been. New sauces for Shawerma may be allowed, but the all-enveloping flatbread remains the same. Although the ancient Egyptians are credited with the discovery of sourdough (finds from around 1800 BC suggest this), it is precisely those countries that went down in history as the first bread bakers that are holding on to the original form of bread. They do not want to let go of their flat bread.

bread seller in Tunisia 2018

They are the most important staple food, go well with everything and are still used everywhere, especially as a substitute for cutlery. At the same time, they are used as edible packaging for delicious combinations of meat, cheese or vegetables.

In the Orient, bread is an essential part of every meal, even when other carbohydrates are served with it. This was also the case in Europe in the past. Bread was and still is considered a gift from God in the Islamic, Christian and Jewish faiths.

The Bible contains many references to grain and bread as food, because man's concern for his "daily bread" dominated thinking in the past.

Every failed harvest called survival into question. This also explains the plea in the Lord's Prayer: "..give us this day our daily bread..". Bread was existential.

As in Europe, there are also numerous rituals and traditions surrounding bread in the eastern countries: breaking bread together is not something you do with just anyone.

Flatbread is the earliest form of bread and is a direct descendant of the oldest grain recipe in the world: porridge. Flatbreads are known in all agricultural cultures and are still the most widespread type of bread worldwide.

Over the millennia, however, improved flours and baking techniques have given rise to exciting and delicious regional variations.

In India and Pakistan, flatbreads (commonly known as roti) come in many varieties, including soft and thick naan, thin chapati, buttery paratha, wholegrain puri and the wafer-thin, usually spicy papadum. Arabic flatbreads are usually very thin, consisting only of a top and bottom crust, and can therefore be opened into a pocket that can be filled with meat and vegetables. The dough does not always contain yeast, and if it does, it is often only a pinch.

Turkey also has a wide variety of breads, from thin yufka sheets to sesame seed rings and many types of filled breads to the several-centimeter-thick pide. The somewhat thinner Greek version of this is called pita. Iran has a darker bread that is traditionally baked on hot pebbles (sangak). In Iran and neighboring countries, the huge thin lavash flatbread is also well known.

Wafer-thin puff pastry sheets similar to Turkish yufka can also be found elsewhere: so-called filyo in Greece (Greek φύλλο = "leaf", also "fillo" or "filo"), in Egypt as gulash or as malsouka in North Africa. Specialties such as spanakopita, galaktoboureko (Greece) or fried dough pockets called brik (North Africa, Tunisia) are made from it.

In Israel, pita is the most popular type of bread today. Unleavened matzo is a special flatbread for the Jewish Passover; the host used in Western churches for Holy Communion/the Eucharist is also a development of this bread.

Of course, flatbread also spread to the northern Mediterranean region; we only have to think of Italy with focaccia, pizza or piadina. Even further north, crispbread and a few other flat breads, such as flatbrauð, a soft pan-baked bread made from whole grain flour in Sweden, or flatbrød in Norway, are reminiscent of the original form. Flatbread is found all over the world!

In Arab culture, it is clear that it is not couscous, tagine, this stew or that casserole that characterizes the national cuisine. Rather, what all countries have in common is that not even a pasta or rice dish is served without bread. Bread is not a side dish. Bread is an integral part of every meal. Often there are dishes that a European would consider just enough for two people. With bread, however, twice as many can be satisfied. The sauce (marqa) is often the (second) most important part, while meat and vegetables act as side dishes.

Bread is so highly regarded in the Islamic world that it is never thrown away. There are separate bags for bread and garbage. Dry bread is collected and then fed to the animals. It is considered a sin to mix it with the garbage.

In view of the overwhelming variety, we begin our expedition in the countries and regions where (flat) bread originated, and we look for typical and exciting recipes there.

photo: Women travel on camels through the Sinai.

Traveling in Morocco

Morocco

Morocco has at least a dozen better-known types of bread, and there are certainly many more that are only baked regionally. Most breads are made from wheat flour and are almost always semi-leavened. Moroccans love their bread firm and with a crust. Many Moroccans do not eat the inside of the bread, preferring only the outside.

The most commonly eaten breads are the round, semi-flat loaves simply called khobz (bread). They can be made from white flour, whole wheat flour, or a mix of different flours. In the past, large, round loaves were made and brought to the community bakery. If you have access to a standard kitchen setup, you can bake them yourself.

While round khobz loaves are most commonly used in everyday life, there are other types of Moroccan bread that are eaten at different times of the day or on different occasions.

In rural areas such as the High Atlas or the Dades Valley, bread is still traditionally baked in a clay tandoor oven.

The wide variety of breads results from the different methods of preparation, the different folding techniques and the spices that are added. Batbout, the "Moroccan pita bread", is the second most popular bread and can easily be made at home in a pan. Mlaoui and Msemmen are almost the same thing; they are just folded differently. They are buttery layered flatbreads that are baked in the pan and are often served for breakfast or as a snack. A variation of this is rghaif shema, flatbreads filled with ground beef or chicken and spices, which are often eaten for supper. They are popular with tourists as "Berber pizza". The Jewish

Moufletta is similar to the msemmen, but is easier to prepare. Moroccan harcha is a kind of pan bread, usually made from semolina. Beghrir are the 1001-hole pancakes that are only baked on one side and are often eaten with honey and butter.

Jewish challah bread is the traditional Shabbat bread of Moroccan Jews. The Sahara, sand or ash bread, which is eaten by all desert dwellers, rounds off the selection.

Moroccan pan baked bread

Khobz – Moroccan flatbread

It is called Khobz, "bread". Some people also call it tagine bread. It is the "classic" Moroccan flatbread that you can get everywhere in Morocco. You can bake it in the oven or on a griddle or in a non-stick pan without fat. It cooks faster in the pan, and rises more in the oven.

Ingredients for 4-6 larger flatbreads
or 8-12 small flatbread rolls
500 g flour
lukewarm water
1 sachet yeast
2 tsp salt
1 tsp sugar
¼ cup vegetable oil

- In a small bowl, combine the yeast, sugar, and a little warm water. Mix well and wait a few minutes for the yeast to bubble.

- In a large bowl or in the food processor, add the flour and salt and stir in the yeast mixture. Have another cup of warm water ready and add it slowly to the flour mixture until the dough can be formed into a ball. At this point, it should be a little sticky.

- Add a little oil to your hands and work it into the dough. Most of the dough should come away from your hands and combine into a dough that is elastic but no longer sticky.

- Knead for 8-10 minutes. This can be done by hand or in a food processor – in a blender, the time is reduced to 5 minutes.

- Oil the dough ball, also the bowl, and cover with cling film. Let rest for 15 minutes.
- Divide the dough into 2-3 portions, depending on the size of the bread you want.
- Form 2-3 smaller balls from the divided pieces.
- Sprinkle flour on a work surface and roll out the balls evenly.
- The dough should be about 6-7 mm thick.
- Cover the rolled out balls with a cloth and let them rest for 45 minutes. Preheat the oven to 220°C.
- Once the dough has risen, prick it several times with a fork. Place on a baking tray (with baking paper) or a hot pizza stone in the oven.
- When the breads are browned and you hear a hollow sound when you tap them, they are ready. This takes about 18-20 minutes, depending on the oven.
- Take them out and let them cool.

Batbout

Batbout bread can be baked in smaller or larger sizes. The smaller ones are very popular with children, even more so when they are filled accordingly. These Moroccan breads are even in demand in Saudi Arabia, especially during Ramadan. There they are called fatout.
If you don't have access to an oven, this Moroccan bread is the solution. Like many other flatbreads, it can be baked on an electric stove in a large pan, preferably cast-iron, or put in the oven. The resting time is very important for this bread. Only then will it be soft and fluffy. This is a flatbread for the tagine, but also a typical breakfast bread. It is often served in private households.

6 medium loaves, many mini loaves or approx. 12 rolls:
500 g flour
100 g finest semolina
½ tsp yeast
½ tsp sugar
1 tsp salt
2-3 tbsp oil
approx. 350 ml lukewarm water
Egg yolk for brushing
opt. caraway, fennel, sesame and paprika for sprinkling

Morocco

Knead a smooth, no longer sticky dough and let it stand covered for 1-2 hours, or even longer if you like.

Buns: twist the balls and press them flat or roll them (approx. 2 cm thick). Bake on both sides in a pan.

• Minis: Roll out the dough to approx. 1 cm thick and cut out into the desired shapes. Leave to rise on the baking tray for at least another hour. Bake in the oven at 200°C or in a hot, grease-free pan until golden brown. They need to be turned in the pan, but not in the oven.

• Rolls: Form into balls, place on the baking sheet at short intervals, brush and sprinkle if necessary, and let rise for another 30 minutes. Then place in the preheated oven at 200° to 230° for 30 minutes and bake until golden brown. After baking, cover with a cloth and place in a plastic bag to keep warm and prevent drying out.

For the bread-shaped Batbout, see page 25.

Above: mini Batbout in the shape of a khamsa.

Msemmen flatbread or snail mlaoui

Msemmen or Mlaoui flatbreads are a popular breakfast and afternoon tea food in Morocco. It's not the easiest bread to make for beginners, but once you get the hang of how it should be textured, it's a breeze. It's definitely worth practicing: kids will gobble it up and eat it without any toppings. It can be served in many different ways, for example with honey and butter instead of savory ingredients. Msemmen are usually square, Mlaoui round.

The Moroccan Mlaoui are similar to the Tunisian Mlaoui pies, but have their own charm due to their snail shape. The Tunisian ones are also made only with semolina and oil.

Ingredients for 6-8 pitta breads
350 g flour
150 g soft wheat semolina
1 pinch of yeast
1 tsp salt
250-275 ml lukewarm water
100-150 g olive oil
100 g melted butter
1 handful of semolina for sprinkling

Tip: my personal favorite consists of half/half semolina and flour, each about 350g, a ¼ P dry yeast and a ¼ tsp baking powder, as well as plenty of half/half olive oil and melted butter.

Two things are important for a successful dough: the water should definitely be lukewarm and the dough is initially mixed without any fat. This results in a soft mass that is kneaded for about 10 minutes. Only then should a little oil be added to prevent the dough from sticking. Then let it rest for 20 minutes. Form balls and let them rest for another 15 minutes. The dough now has an elastic consistency that is somewhat reminiscent of memory foam.

Mix the butter and oil in a small bowl. Flatten the balls with your hands and pull them apart, working in plenty of the oil and butter mixture.

Now the steps for Msemmen and Mlaoui vary:

- For the **Mlaoui,** fold the dough in half from two sides (one above the other), then fold the long side to form a narrow roll, press flat, butter again and roll up crosswise to form a snail. Arrange and flatten half of the snail, set aside and let rest until all balls have been processed in this way.

Start again with the first piece of dough: Now press the snail completely flat again with your hands and roll it out into a circle, 2 to 5 mm thick.

Tip: the one-handed dough roller has proven very useful for this.

Then place in a preheated, coated and grease-free pan (or bake on the baking plate) and bake on a high heat until golden brown on both sides. After turning, press down the edges to ensure that they are also baked all the way through.

Stack the pancakes on a plate, cover with a cloth and put in a plastic bag to keep them warm and soft.

For the **Msemmen,** butter the rolled out dough again and sprinkle with a little fine semolina. Fold in one side, butter, sprinkle, fold over the other side, butter, sprinkle. Now fold in the narrow side, butter, sprinkle, then the other narrow side over it. Turn the resulting "package" with the "seam" downwards (see drawing on page 40).

Then press the packages flat again with oil/butter and roll out, forming square flatbreads. Bake these in a pan on both sides.

The semolina sprinkled on top gives the flatbreads several layers, similar to puff pastry

How to fold the Msemmen:

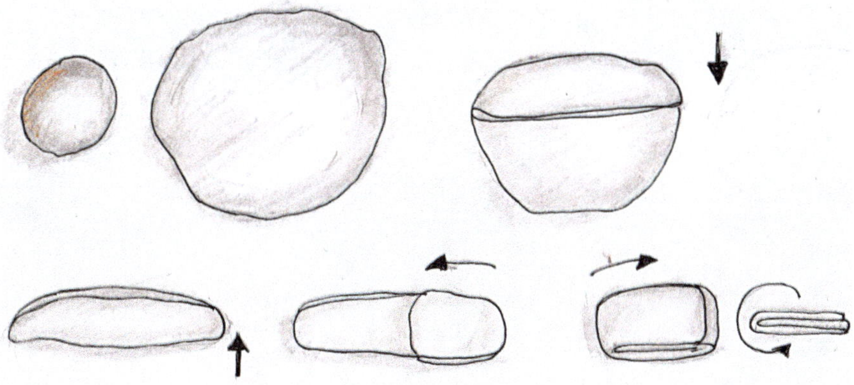

Top: Snail Mlaoui, Bottom: Msemmen

Matlou – Khobz Tajine

The typical tagine or pan bread is also available in Algeria.

Zutaten

For 7-10 pita breads

400 g flour

300 g semolina

1 sachet (dry) yeast

1 tsp salt

1 pinch of sugar

300-350 ml water

- Knead all ingredients, cover and let rise for 30 minutes. Divide into seven to ten pieces and form each into a 1 cm thick flatbread.
- Let rise for another 15-30 minutes.
- Bake in a pan/on a baking plate at high heat for about 4 minutes on each side.

Khobz tajine and Khobz el dar (below)

Khobz el dar – Algerian house bread

If you prefer to make your bread in the oven, try the following recipe for a light bread made from flour and semolina. The so-called "black sesame" is the seed of the blessing grain (Arabic: Habet el baraka), black cumin or Latin: Nigella sativa.

Black cumin has a beneficial effect on digestion and, like the oil of the same name, is used for a variety of ailments.

Ingredients for a 18 cm springform pan
100 g soft wheat semolina
1 tsp salt
1 tbsp sugar
½ sachet of dry yeast
1 tbsp white sesame seeds
1 tbsp black sesame seeds
4 tbsp olive or rapeseed oil
1 egg
1 egg white
250 ml milk, lukewarm
350 g flour + flour for kneading
For sprinkling:
sesame seeds, white
1 egg yolk

- Mix all the ingredients except the flour in a bowl and let it rise for about 2 hours until it starts to ferment.
- Stir in the flour. The dough is very sticky. Let it rise in a warm place

for about an hour, until it has doubled in volume.

- Tip: This "pre-dough" can easily be made the day before and left to rise in the refrigerator overnight.
- Sprinkle a little flour on the dough and dust your hands with flour. Add flour by the tablespoonful until the dough comes away from the sides of the bowl and can be shaped into a ball.
- Tip: It's easier to do in a food processor.
- Line an 18 cm springform pan with baking paper. Grease the edge a little. Place the dough ball in the pan and press it into the mold. Let rise for 1 hour. Preheat the oven to 230°C.
- Carefully brush the egg yolk onto the dough using a brush and sprinkle with a little sesame seeds. Bake in a preheated oven at 230°C for about 30-40 minutes, until the top is golden yellow. Leave to cool on a cake rack.

Tunisia

Tunisian bread, also known as "Khobz Tounes", is an integral and important part of every meal in Tunisia. Traditionally, it was baked in a special wooden oven called "Tabouna", which has a conical shape. In the past, the women of the family would gather to prepare the dough and shape the bread, while the men stoked the fire in the oven and baked the bread. With the French colonization, the baguette found its way into Tunisian cuisine and has largely replaced the local bread. With the increase in the number of women in employment, the labor-intensive home baking of bread has declined more and more, and so today you can meet younger Tunisian women who have never baked kessra or mlaoui.

Kessra

There are special baking tins for kessra, the typical Tunisian pan bread. It is quicker and more even in the shallow iron pan with grooves. In the clay pot, you have to be very careful that it does not burn in the middle, because the pot is not flat, unlike the metal forms. To ensure that the bread is also baked all the way around, you turn it a little bit each time. Some people find that the bread tastes better when baked in a clay pot because it takes longer and the bread rises a little more during baking.

If you don't have either of these, you should use a suitable pan, preferably made of cast iron and with a non-stick coating. This will work just as well.

Tunisia

Ingredients for approx. 6-8 loaves

500 g fine semolina

100 g flour

1 sachet of dry yeast

1 tsp salt

1 tsp sugar

2 tbsp olive oil

lukewarm water

- Mix the dry ingredients well. Then add enough water to create a dough that is not too firm but elastic. Form balls the size of an apple and leave to rise in a warm place for 1 hour, covered.

- Now roll out the dough to about 16/18 cm (diameter) and 1 cm thick and let it rise again for 1 hour, covered.

- Bake on a low heat on both sides without fat, not forgetting the edge. Place the finished bread in a flat dish, cover with a cloth and put in a plastic bag to keep it warm and soft.

Kessra out of the clay pot and out of the iron pan

Kessra Mlaoui

They resemble the Moroccan Mlaoui, but here the dough is made only from fine semolina (smid rutub). In addition to water and salt, a fair amount of olive oil is added until the dough is pliable. You can eat the bread with honey or sugar for breakfast, or with olive oil and Harissa arbi for dinner, i.e. not with the ready-made Harissa from the can that you would otherwise use for cooking, but with homemade Harissa, which is also called "Haruss" to distinguish it and is even spicier and more aromatic.

This freshly baked flatbread is also delicious with many other meals, such as kamounia (a meat, liver or fish dish with lots of onions and cumin), shorba (soup), and any kind of marqa (sauce). Children prefer to eat it warm out of the pan, without any topping. Two large flatbreads are enough to feed one person.

Ingredients for the dough (enough for 8-9 pieces)
700-800 g fine semolina
salt
1/3 sachet of dry yeast
lukewarm water
olive oil

- Mix the dough with lukewarm (!) water. Knead in the food processor for 10 minutes. If you knead for too short a time, the pita bread will not be pliable later, but rather brittle.

- Then add ½-1 small cup of oil by the spoonful.

- Knead vigorously for another 5 minutes in the food processor or with oiled hands on an oiled surface. Keep dipping your hands in oil, pulling the dough apart, drizzling with a little oil and working it in.

- • When it is nice and pliable, form small balls and let them rest for 20 minutes. Then flatten the balls, pull them apart with your hands, almost like rolling out dough. Add more oil if necessary.

- • Now fold a small package: Fold the right side towards the middle, fold the left side towards the middle and place it over the right side. Now do the same lengthwise: Fold from the top towards the middle and fold the lower half back over the top. Turn over so that the smooth side is facing up. Now make such folded packages out of all the balls (see illustrations). Then let the packages rest for a few more minutes so that they hold their shape better when stretched out.

- Heat the baking plate (or pan).

- Now start again with the first package: roll it out again from the middle and press it flat with freshly oiled hands until the dough is evenly thick, about the size of a thick pancake and the size of the pan it is to be in. You will soon find out the right thickness. Too thin a dough makes the pancakes brittle and they dry out quickly; if they are too thick, they taste doughy. They should be a mixture of soft and crispy and, after baking (and a few hours later), can be tossed like rags.

- Place the patties quickly but carefully in the hot pan. Cook the first side. When the patty has become stable and the baking side is brown, turn the patties over.

- .With an oiled cloth (or another suitable object), press the dough onto the bottom, especially at the edge, so that all areas are baked through; the thicker edges are especially important.

- Stack them on a plate, cover with a cloth and put them in a plastic bag to keep them warm and soft for a long time.
- The flatbreads taste best when warm, but they are also very tasty cold. You can heat them briefly in a pan the next day, and they will be almost as good as fresh.
- Tip: I use an oiled cloth or a paper towel holder to press the dough, especially at the edges, onto the bottom.

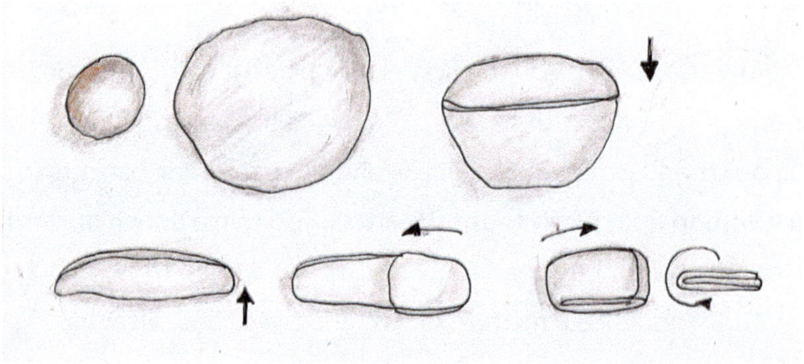

Folding Mlaoui „parcel“

Tabouna –the Phoenician bread

Tabouna is the name of the oven that the ancient Carthaginians called "tannour". The term is confirmed in both Arabic and Hebrew. It comes from the Arabic word taboun, which refers to the hearth fire, and the verb tabana means "stoking the fire". Remains of tannour ovens from 800 BC have been found in Spain. Tannour ovens were tubular – they come in both vertical and horizontal varieties – and the dough patties were slapped against the hot oven wall on the inside. This created a delicate smoky flavor that is of course absent when baking in an electric oven.

There are only a few households left that own such an oven or have the time and wood to heat it. Nowadays, however, there are Tabouna ovens that are heated by gas.

While the bread used to be made from wholemeal flour and started with sourdough, today it is made from white flour, sugar, salt, yeast and olive oil. This makes it much more puffy than the original. It has a round shape and is often decorated with sesame seeds on top. The bread is served with hot dishes such as shakshuka and scrambled eggs in tomato sauce or egg in Olivenöl getaucht und pur genossen.

Ingredients for 4 loaves of bread, each weighing about 400 g

500 g semolina
500 g flour

2 sachets of dry yeast or 1 cube of fresh yeast
1 tbsp sugar
1 tbsp salt
2 heaped tbsp soft butter or margarine
4 tbsp olive oil
lukewarm water

Topping
1 egg, beaten
toasted sesame seeds

- Preheat the oven to 200°C top/bottom heat. First mix the dry ingredients, then gradually add the water and knead until a smooth dough is formed. You will need a little more water than with a pure flour dough because of the semolina.
- Cover and leave to rise in a warm place for 1 hour.
- Then form four equal-sized, round loaves. Place on the baking tray and let rise for another 15 minutes.
- Brush with the beaten egg, cut a lattice pattern into the dough and sprinkle with sesame seeds.
- Bake on the bottom rack for about 20 to 25 minutes.
- Let cool before slicing.
- Tip: Freeze any bread that is overbaked, defrost as needed and briefly place in the oven again.

Tabouna made with the electric oven

Fetir – filled yeast doughnuts

In Tunisia, they are called "Turkish pancakes". They taste delicious, are very popular and – as is unfortunately often the case – are also very rich.

The dough is quite similar to that of Hungarian lángos. In principle, they can be filled with anything you have to hand: spinach and feta, vegetables, minced meat and much more. Cheese is always a good choice.

Ingredients for 12 pieces
120 ml water
120 ml milk
1/2 packet dry yeast
1 tablespoon salt
1 tablespoon olive oil
1 tablespoon sugar
400-450 g flour
oil for frying

Filling: as you like, e.g. :
2 tomatoes, finely diced
4 green pointed peppers, finely chopped
2 onions, finely chopped
4 garlic cloves, pressed
1 can of tuna
1 good handful of grated cheese
(Mozarella, goat's cheese, Gouda, Gruyere etc)
Coriander, cumin, salt, pepper for 12 units

- Knead a smooth, soft dough from the ingredients. Use as much flour as necessary, but it should remain soft. Leave to rise in a warm place for 30 minutes.

- Steam the onions until translucent, crush the garlic with 1 tablespoon of coriander in a mortar and add. Add the paprika and tomatoes, cover and steam until soft. Add the tomatoes, simmer until the juice has evaporated, add the tuna, season. Leave to cool.

- • Make small balls out of the dough, press them apart a little, add 1 tablespoon of cooled filling, sprinkle with cheese, close well.

- Now gently press this "dough bag" flat and "massage" it a little so that the dough and filling mix a little. Fry in a pan with a little neutral oil until golden brown on both sides and then drain on kitchen paper. They taste best when lukewarm.

Fricassé – filled, fried yeast rolls

If you're thinking of chicken fricassee, you're way off. Nobody knows how this sandwich got its name. In any case, it is a "typically Tunisian" filled fried yeast roll. Typically Tunisian means: potatoes, tuna and eggs as the main ingredients. Very tasty, very filling, very popular.

Ingredients for 8-10 pieces
500 g flour
1 P dry yeast
1 tsp sugar
some lukewarm water
1 egg yolk
1/2 glass of olive oil
pinch of salt

For the filling:
4-6 hard-boiled eggs, halved or quartered
black or green olives, pitted
1can of tuna or meat sausage (Tunisian "salami")
harissa
3-4 potatoes boiled in salted water, mashed, seasoned with a little cumin and lemon
optional "deluxe": Slata Meshwiya or from 5 tomatoes, 3 green peppers, 1-2 garlic cloves, cumin and salt in olive oil, simmered, chunky

Shakshuka sauce,

capers optional. ones

- Mix all the dry ingredients for the dough. Then stir in the olive oil and egg yolk and enough water to create an elastic dough. Cover and let rise in a warm place for 30 minutes.

- Take small balls out of the dough, form oval and very flat (!) rolls and fry them in plenty of hot oil on both sides relatively slowly so that they are also cooked on the inside. Let them drain on kitchen paper, let them cool, cut them lengthwise (but do not cut them through) and then fill them. First spread harissa on both sides, then spread the potatoes on one half, add a little tuna on top, 2 quarters of a boiled egg, the sauce, olives and, if you like, some capers.

- Tip: Do not make the dough pieces thicker than 2 cm and keep the oil on a low heat (hot, but not smoking). It takes longer, but experience shows that if either the dough piece is too thick or the frying fat is too hot, the inside is still doughy and the outside is already black.

Fricassé

Shami – Pizza-Wraps

In Tunisia, delicious wraps are called shami – which is actually the Arabic term for the countries of Syria, Palestine, Jordan and Lebanon. Sometimes you will also see "Lebanese" on the menu. This popular fast food has spread throughout North Africa with the Syrian refugee flow via Egypt. However, instead of being made from light, soft pita bread, in Tunisia they are made from crispy pizza dough and fried on both sides in a pan before being briefly put in the oven for the finale.

Ingredients for 6 shami
Pizza dough made from
600 g flour
1 sachet of dry yeast
1 teaspoon of sugar
1 teaspoon of salt
2 tablespoons of olive oil
tepid water flauwarmes Wasser

- Mix all ingredients, knead well, cover and leave to rise in a warm place for 1 hour.
- Tip: You can also prepare the pizza dough 1 or 2 days in advance and leave it to rise in the fridge.

Filling:

Tomato sauce made from

2 large tomatoes

1 tsp tomato puree

1 tsp salt

1/2 tsp sugar

1/2 tsp cumin

1 small onion

2 cloves of garlic

2-3 cups of water

Olive oil

- Mix all the ingredients, knead well, cover and leave to rise in a warm place for 1 hour.
- Tip: You can also prepare the pizza dough a day or two in advance and leave it to rise in the fridge.

Additional ingredients for the filling:

300 g chicken meat in small pieces, grilled or fried (tip: marinate in soy sauce beforehand)

1 iceberg lettuce, cut into broad strips

3-4 grated carrots

tomatoes, cut into slices

cucumbers, cut into large lengthwise strips

Grated mozzarella or other hard cheese that melts well

Various sauces: ketchup, cocktail sauce, mayonnaise

Freshly fried French fries

- Preheat the oven (fan-assisted with grill). Preheat the pan. Divide the pizza dough into 6 balls.
- Roll out 1 cm thinly. Bake on the baking plate or in a large cast-iron pan on both sides.
- While the 2nd side is baking, spread a thin layer of tomato sauce on the top side.
- Place 2-3 tablespoons of meat in the middle, remove from heat.
- If you don't want to heat the salad, then add some fries and more cheese on top and put it back in the preheated oven for a few minutes.
- Then top with your favorite sauces, carrots, iceberg lettuce, cucumbers and tomato slices. Close, don't think about the calories and enjoy.
-

Libya

Tuareg Bread Tgilla

The ash bread, known as Khobza al Malla in Arabic, is well known throughout the Middle East and was also known in Europe during the Middle Ages. Nowadays, Bedouins who travel through the desert with camels also use old satellite dishes that are placed over the hot embers. This allows them to bake thinner rolled-out dough patties that cook much faster. Empty tin cans are often used as rollers.

Knead a smooth dough from flour, water and salt and let it rest for 20 minutes. Then make a flatbread about 4 centimeters thick and place it in the hot ash. Turn it over after about 20 minutes.

Egypt

In all Arabic countries, bread is simply called khobz. Except in Egypt, where it is called ***aisch***, a word meaning "life". This alone shows how essential it is to the Egyptians. The most popular type of flatbread is aisch baladi, the traditional country bread. Even those who have hardly anything can still eat aisch baladi with a few onions and rocket. As in all of the Orient, it is used as a dipping bread for sauces and creamy "salads" and as a substitute for cutlery: you tear off a piece and fold it like a cat's ear, "widn el otta".

There are numerous types of bread in the land of the Nile. Some papier-mâché versions of them are on display in dusty display cases in a kind of local history museum in Cairo.

The most important types of bread in Egypt, however, are Aisch baladi, the country bread, and Aisch shams, the sun bread.

Aisch baladi has a higher bran content than the Aisch schami, which is also available. The latter is a Lebanese flatbread (schami is the name of the region of Lebanon, Jordan, Syria, Palestine). It is therefore not quite as suitable for filling as the light-colored Aisch schami. The light-colored version is also available (at least in Germany) as "Arabic flatbread".

Aisch baladi – Country bread

Ingredients for 10-12 pita breads
500 g wheat flour
(you can also use half each
whole wheat flour and white flour)
2 sachets of dry yeast
1 tsp sugar
1 tsp salt
250 to 280 ml lukewarm water
approx. 100 g bran

- Mix the flour with half of the bran, add the yeast and salt, and knead for 10 minutes. Then cover and leave to rise in a warm place for 2 hours.
- Spread the remaining bran on the work surface.

- Form about tennis ball-sized balls from the part 10-12 and roll out to 5 mm thick circles. Sprinkle all the flatbreads with bran. Leave to rest for 30 minutes.

- Preheat the oven to the highest temperature, tray and, if necessary, pizza stone as well. Place the flatbread on the hot tray.

- The baking time varies depending on the oven. With a hot air oven or a good oven with a pizza stone (approx. 300°), it takes about 5 minutes. At a lower temperature, it takes correspondingly longer. The bread should inflate like a balloon. As soon as slight wrinkles form at the edge, the bread is ready.

- Pile on a plate, cover with a cloth and keep warm and soft in a plastic bag.

Aish baladi

Aish eShams – Sun bread

It is best to prepare a starter dough the day before if you want to make large, round, sun-dried bread. This is because the bread will need a few hours to rise and rest the next day as well, depending on the temperature.

In Egypt, it is common to scrape the leftover dough out of the bowl and freeze it for use in the next batch of starter dough.

Pre-ferment:
thawed dough scraps from the last baking day
1 cup flour
1 cup lukewarm water
1 sachet dry yeast
2 teaspoons sugar
1 teaspoon salt

Dough:
350 g flour
Pre-ferment
bran:

- Mix the ingredients to a liquid starter dough, cover with cling film and leave to stand in the refrigerator overnight.

- The next morning, mix 350 g of flour with the starter dough and add enough lukewarm water to form a loose, soft and sticky dough. You can knead the bread better with bran on your hands.

- Form one large loaf or two smaller ones. Sprinkle bran on a large plate and place the dough ball on it. Flatten the dough ball and let it rise for 3-4 hours until it has doubled in volume.

- Preheat the oven to the highest temperature: 230°C or higher. If necessary, switch on the grill function as well. If you have the bread in the oven, switch off the grill function again.

- Now use a pin to make small incisions all around the edge of the dough at the bottom to allow the air to escape. Place the bread on a baking tray lined with baking paper and bake until it has turned a light brown color. If it sounds hollow when you tap it, it is sure to be baked through on the inside as well.

- Remove from the oven and allow to cool slightly before slicing.

Hawauschi – filled dumplings

We were in Aswan, wandering the streets early in the morning looking for a breakfast cafe. And we found these super-delicious pastries, freshly prepared before our eyes. I later learned that Hawauschi was invented in Cairo in 1971 by a butcher named Ahmed al-Hawausch. After his death, the recipe spread throughout Egypt and did what recipes do: it changed. While it was initially just a filling in pita bread that was baked, fresh yeast dough was soon added in the Nile Delta and Alexandria. So, in addition to the "Alexandria Style" and the "Cairo Style", there are now a number of other rolls that are spiced or packaged differently from region to region.

Ingredients for about 8 pasties
500 g flour
1 sachet yeast
1 tsp salt
1 tsp sugar
250 ml lukewarm water
2-4 tbsp oil
100 g yoghurt

Filling
500 g ground beef or lamb
2 large onions, finely chopped
2 cloves of garlic, pressed

1 red bell pepper, in large pieces
1/2 bunch parsley, finely chopped
salt, pepper
teaspoon chili or hot red pepper powder
1 teaspoon cumin powder
oil for frying

- Prepare soft dough, let rise in warm place for 1 hour.
- Fry the onions in hot oil. Add the minced meat.
- Add the bell pepper and garlic. Season.
- When the bell pepper is soft, season with parsley.
- Twist off balls and roll out into flat discs.
- Put 1-3 tablespoons of filling in the middle, press the edges together to form a "bag" and twist it, then gently press it flat.
- If necessary, carefully flatten it with a hand roller.
- Deep-fry in hot fat on both sides, then drain.

Yemen

Kubaneh – Jewish-Yemeni Sabbath bread

For once, not a flatbread. These delicious yeast rolls are buttery and flaky, crispy on the outside and fluffy on the inside, not unlike a croissant.

Traditionally, they are baked overnight at a low temperature so that they are ready for breakfast on Sabbath morning. There are special ovens with a Sabbath setting for this purpose. But the bread turns out wonderfully in a normal oven. If you want, you can make a pre-dough from 100 g flour, 100 ml water and the packet of yeast and leave it to rise in the fridge overnight. In principle, yeast dough becomes more tender and fluffier as a result. But a sufficiently long resting time is enough to make it rise.

In addition to the sweet version, you can also make a savory one, which is served with Yemeni Schug (a hot spicy paste) instead of honey.

Without pre-ferment

500 g flour

300 g water

1 sachet yeast

2 tbsp sugar (only 1 tsp for the savory version) Vorteig

500 g flour

300 g water

1 sachet yeast

2 tbsp sugar (only 1 tsp for the savory version)

1 tsp salt

150 g butter, very soft to liquid

with pre-ferment

Pre-ferment plus 400 g flour

200 g water

2 tablespoons sugar (only 1 teaspoon for the savory version)

1 teaspoon salt

150 g liquid or very soft butter

- Knead the ingredients except the butter into a smooth dough. Keep pulling the mixture from the inside out and working it back in. Turn the dough ball a little until you have an even ball. Place in a buttered bowl and let rise in a warm place for 2 hours.
- Grease a round springform pan with butter.
- Preheat the oven to 175°.
- Form 8 balls out of the dough.
- Pull the balls apart with your hands and spread them out, working in plenty of butter. Fold in from two sides, then fold into a long roll and wrap this up into a snail shape. Cut in half and place in the springform pan with the cut surface facing upwards. Leave to rise again until all the snails are touching.
- Brush with plenty of butter again.

- Bake for 15 minutes, then reduce the heat slightly and bake for another 30 minutes until the rosettes are golden brown.

- The sweet version can be sprinkled with cinnamon sugar or date sugar before baking.

- Alternatively, you can make a savory version. In this case, use only 1 teaspoon of sugar for the dough. After rolling out and brushing with butter, sprinkle the dough with Zatar (thyme mixture) and "black sesame" (black cumin seeds), then fold and roll up into a rosette.

- Brush the finished rosettes with butter before baking and sprinkle with white sesame seeds

- It can be stored covered with a plastic bag and heats up quickly (e.g. in the Airfryer) to taste like fresh again.

Syria & Jordan

Arabic pancake bread from the pan

500 g flour
1 tsp sugar
1 sachet yeast
1 tsp salt
1 tbsp oil
250 g lukewarm water
opt. ¼ tsp mixed caraway seeds

- Let the dough rise for 2 hours and then form 12 balls. Roll these out into flat circles about the thickness of a pancake and let them rest again for 5-10 minutes. Then bake them in a hot pan or on the baking plate. Turn them once so that they get some color on both sides.

- You can also make the bread without yeast, in which case a resting time of 30 minutes is enough. Of course, it will be flatter as a result.

Lebanon

Flatbread from the oven – for filling and for wraps

In Lebanon, the popular wraps are called "wrapped brides" and, like everywhere in the Arab world, this type of fast food is very popular.

500 g flour
1 sachet of yeast
1 teaspoon sugar
320 ml lukewarm water
80 ml olive oil

- Knead the ingredients by hand for 10 minutes or by machine for 5 minutes. They produce a soft, sticky dough, which can be worked very well with additional flour on the hands. Leave to rise for 1-2 hours. Turn out 8 balls and leave to relax again for 15 minutes, covered.

- Preheat the oven and baking tray (a pizza stone is even better) to 250° O/U. Roll out the ball into 2 mm thick circles and bake on the hot baking tray for 2-7 minutes (depending on the oven). Ideally, the bottom and top crusts will separate and the bread will puff up into a balloon.

- For those who like it filled: the resulting cavity can be filled with anything your heart desires: grilled meat along with- various sauces, grilled haloumi cheese, falafel, salad, chips with mayo and ketchup, etc.

- Cover the breads with a cloth and then wrap them in a plastic bag to keep them soft and elastic.

- Like other flatbreads, these can also be baked in a pan, but then the top and bottom crusts do not separate, meaning that the bread does not puff up into a balloon. However, you can still wrap delicious ingredients in the soft, flat bread.

Iraq

Samoun – Traditional flatbread in diamond shape

It is one of our favorite breads: fluffy and not dry. Traditionally baked in the tandoor, it is preferably served with Gaimar cream (available on the Internet; alternatively cream cheese) or eaten with cheese. But whether as a sandwich or with soup, it always tastes good.

480 g flour
½ cup wheat bran
½ tsp sugar
1 teaspoon salt
225 ml buttermilk
2 tsp oil
1.5 tsp yeast
1 cup lukewarm water (200 ml)

For coating: Egg yolk mixed with a little water
To sprinkle: sesame seeds

- Knead a smooth dough and leave to rise for 1 hour until the dough has doubled in size.
- Turn out 4 balls and leave to rest for a further 10 minutes.

- Now roll and pull flat into a diamond shape, place on baking paper and leave to rest for another 30 minutes. Preheat the oven to 230°. Brush with egg and water, sprinkle with sesame seeds and bake for 15 to 18 minutes until golden brown, depending on the oven.

Mossul bread from Kurdistan

Ingredients for 8 rolls

550 g wheat flour

240 g lukewarm water

50 ml oil

1 tsp. dry yeast

1 tsp. sugar

1 tsp. salt

1 tsp. black cumin

opt. 1 tsp. ground fennel seeds

For brushing/sprinkling

1 egg, beaten

30 g sesame seeds

- In a small bowl, dissolve the sugar and yeast in lukewarm water and let it ferment for 15 minutes.

- Mix the flour, spices and salt in a bowl. Add the oil, lukewarm water and yeast mixture and knead for 5 minutes with a food processor. The result should be a smooth, non-sticky yeast dough.

- Form a ball, brush with a little oil, cover the bowl with a cloth and leave the bread dough to rise in a warm place for 1 hour.

- Knead the dough briefly and divide into equal-sized pieces.

- For 8 small rolls, divide the dough into balls of approx. 100 g each, or for 4 small loaves, divide into pieces of approx. 200 g each and shape into elongated rolls/loaves.

- Place the dough pieces on a baking tray lined with baking paper, cover with a cloth and leave to rise in a warm place for a further 30 minutes.

- Use a knife to score the top of the loaves/rolls in a diamond pattern, brush with the beaten egg and sprinkle generously with black cumin and/or sesame seeds.

- Bake in a preheated oven (160°C/320°F; fan-assisted) on the middle shelf for 20-40 minutes until golden brown.

Mossulbrot aus Kurdistan

Kurdish Kalâneh –fried stuffed flatbreads

They are very tasty and, like everywhere, can be prepared with different fillings, including vegetables and minced meat.

This classic filling with spring onions is particularly popular. The brown butter makes the bread particularly delicious. In some regions, the word kalâneh is not only used for flatbreads but also for a musical instrument.

Ingredients for the dough
320 g flour
1 tsp salt
1 tsp oil
160 ml lukewarm water

Filling
80 g salted butter, browned
2 bunches spring onions, finely chopped
opt. brined cheese/feta/ricotta

- Knead a smooth dough, brush the dough ball with oil or wrap it in cling film and let it rest in a warm place for 30 minutes.
- Then roll out 4-6 balls into thin circles.
- Cover half of them with chopped spring onions, fold them up and press the edges firmly.
- Dust the bread with flour, fry in and brush with browned butter.

Kalâneh

Turkey

Pide – Ramazan Pidesi flatbread

The crust made from egg, flour and sesame seeds gives this flat-bread its special flavor: crispy on the outside, fluffy on the inside. It turns out best when the dough is made a day in advance and allowed to rise overnight.

Ingredients for 2 smaller pide:
600 g flour
1 sachet of dry yeast
1 teaspoon of sugar
1 teaspoon of salt
1 egg yolk
1 half glass of olive oil
lukewarm water

For the icing:
1 egg yolk
1 tbsp flour
a little cold water
a little boiling water
sesame seeds

- Mix the dough ingredients to a light, rather sticky dough. Do not knead for too long.

- Oil with olive oil and place in an oiled bowl.
- Cover with cling film and place in the refrigerator overnight.
- The next day, place the dough on the floured work surface and divide into two portions.
- The dough should not be firm, but rather soft and squishy.
- Form an elongated loaf out of each piece of dough using a folding and scooping motion and place it on a baking tray lined with baking paper.
- Flatten the loaves into an oval shape and let them rest for a while.
- In the meantime, prepare the glaze: mix 1 tablespoon of flour with a little cold water until smooth, add a little boiling water and stir. Finally, stir in the egg yolk.
- Brush the flatbreads with it. Then use your fingertips to press a few pattern grooves into the bread: first a ring around the outer edge, then two longitudinal grooves and three diagonal cross grooves, so that a diamond pattern is created. If necessary, brush a little more icing on top. Now sprinkle with the sesame seeds.
- Put in the preheated oven (at least 230°) and bake for 15-30 minutes, depending on the oven. The crust should be golden brown.
- Let it cool down a bit on a wire rack, but it's best to serve it fresh.

Pide

Simmit – sesame seed rings

Every visitor to Istanbul is familiar with them: the "hawkers" with their poles on which fragrant simmit rings are strung. They are the perfect breakfast on the way to the ferry to Üsküdar. Enjoy them with a strong black tea, which you can buy on the ship. The following recipe is recommended for that holiday feeling at home. Instead of being dipped into boiling soda like Bavarian pretzels, the Simmit rings are only dipped into water.

Ingredients for 8-10 pieces
500 g flour
50 g butter, melted
1 sachet of dry yeast
1 tsp salt
2 tsp sugar
1 egg yolk
250 ml lukewarm water
approx. 10 g sesame seeds per spiral
oil for hands and baking tray

- Knead all ingredients by hand for 10 minutes or in a food processor for 5 minutes. Oil the dough, cover and leave to rise in a warm place for 1 hour.

- Roll out into 8-10 balls, roll into dough snakes and close them into rings or drill a hole in the balls and carefully expand it into a ring.

- Dip the dough rings into very hot water for 10 seconds using a slotted spoon. Place on the baking tray, brush with egg and sprinkle with sesame seeds.

- Preheat the oven to approx. 180°.
- Allow the finished dough pieces to rise for 15 minutes until the oven has heated up.
- Then bake in the oven for approx. 25 minutes until golden brown.

Simmit

Lahmacun –Turkish pizza

It is not clear whether this pizza originated in Armenia or Turkey. The name Lahmacun is of Arabic origin and comes from "Lahm bil ajina", which translates as "meat with dough". We know it as a Turkish specialty that is traditionally served with minced meat, onion slices and a lemon wedge. The pita is sprinkled with lemon juice, optionally spiced with Pul Biber (chili flakes), sprinkled with chopped flat-leaf parsley, rolled up and eaten out of the hand. You can also top it with yogurt, finely chopped spicy green peppers, tomatoes, lettuce and cheese.

Ingredients for the dough (12-14 pieces)

700 g flour

2 sachets yeast

1 tbsp sugar

1 tbsp salt

450 ml lukewarm water

50 ml olive oil

Flour for the work surface

Ingredients for the topping (enough for about 20 pizzas; you can freeze half as a supply)

3 red pointed peppers

4 large tomatoes

2 onions

1 large bunch flat-leaf parsley
2-4 garlic cloves
500 g ground beef
2 Tbsp. paprika puree
2 tsp. sweet paprika powder
1 Tbsp. salt
½ tsp. black pepper
1 tsp. chili flakes
2 Tbsp. tomato paste
cumin

- In a small bowl, dissolve the yeast and sugar in the lukewarm water and leave to ferment for 15 minutes. In a large bowl, mix the dry ingredients. Add the oil and stir in the yeast water. Knead the dough until it is nice and smooth but still slightly sticky. Cover with a damp kitchen towel and leave to rise in a warm place for 1 ½ hours.

- During this time, the vegetable-meat paste for the topping is prepared. To do this, the vegetables and parsley are cleaned, roughly chopped and then blended. The vegetable mix is then mixed with the spices and the minced meat and placed in the refrigerator until further processing.

- After the rising time, the dough is formed into 12-14 equal-sized balls and placed on a board or tray dusted with flour. Cover with a cloth or film to prevent dry skin from forming. Leave to rise for a further 30 minutes.

- Preheat the oven to 220-230°C along with the baking tray.

- After the 2nd rising time, the dough balls are rolled out thinly and thinly coated with the paste. Baking time approx. 5-6 minutes. Every oven is different: the times may vary.

- Tip: I first place the dough on the hot baking plate (or pan) so that the base is cooked and crispy; I then spread the filling on top. After a few minutes, I slide the pizza into the oven.

Lepenje – small pita bread

These small flatbreads are made with baking powder instead of yeast.

You can make lepenje in a pan or in the oven using a pizza stone. We love the ones from the pan. They are delicious when fresh and go well with all kinds of things, from cheese, sausage, salad, green onions, sour cream to Spanish potato omelettes and much more.

Ingredients for approx. 12 pieces
350 g wheat flour or
200 g wheat flour and 50 g rye flour
1 sachet baking powder
1 pinch of sugar
1 tsp salt
1 pinch of pepper
250 ml lukewarm milk
Flour for kneading and rolling out
Oil for frying

- Knead a smooth dough (it is a bit sticky) and let it rest for 30 minutes in a warm place, covered with flour. Then form 12 balls of 50 g each and roll them out with a rolling pin until they are circular and flat.
- Heat the oil in a non-stick or cast-iron pan and bake the patties

on both sides.

- I use a non-stick mini pan about 12 cm in diameter (or two at the same time), brush it with olive oil, bake one side and brush the pan and/or the top side of the pancake with oil before turning; if necessary, rinse out the burnt flour from time to time.

Lepenje

Samuna -flat bread roll

A very tasty bread. The dough is quite sticky and a little difficult to work with. It works best with disposable gloves, lots of flour or well-oiled hands.

Ingredients for 12 flatbreads:
1 kg flour
400 ml milk
400 ml water
1 sachet of dry yeast
1 tbsp salt
1 tsp sugar
1 tbsp oil

1Zum Bestreichen: 1 Eigelb mit Wasser verquirlt

Zum Bestreuen: Sesam oder Schwarzkümmel

- Knead the ingredients for 10 minutes, then leave to rise in an oiled bowl for 1.5 hours.
- Place the very soft dough on a floured board and carefully shape into an elongated form. Divide into approx. 12 equal-sized pieces and shape them into balls.
- Cover and let rest for 20 minutes.

- Use your fingertips to “squeeze” the gas outwards from the inside, leaving lots of dents on the pancake. Place on a floured baking sheet. Brush with the water and egg mixture, prick a few times with a fork and sprinkle with sesame seeds or nigella seeds.

- Leave to rest for 20 minutes.

- Tip: You can also add slices of spicy garlic sausage or chunks of sheep's cheese to the rolls for a special flavor.

- Bake in an oven preheated to 250°C until light golden brown.

- Do not bake for too long, as the bread will lose its typical crumb. your fingertips to stretch the dough from the inside out.

Matnakasch – Armenian sourdough flatbread

Nowadays, you can simply make bread with yeast, but in the past, neither fresh nor dry yeast was available for purchase. Sourdough was used as a leavening agent, and this is the original recipe. Sourdough bread has the advantage of staying fresh longer than yeast bread. If you don't have sourdough, use yeast instead and at least make a pre-ferment.

400 g flour, 100 g sourdough, ½ sachet of yeast
or
500 g flour, 1 sachet of yeast
1.5 tsp salt, ½ tsp sugar
350 ml lukewarm water
3 tbsp olive oil
a little flour and cold water

Sourdough bread:

Mix the sourdough with the remaining ingredients and knead by hand for 15 minutes until it is soft and elastic. It should not stick. Cover and leave to rise in a warm place for 2-3 hours.

:

Yeast bread:

Mix the yeast with the sugar and 250 ml of lukewarm water and leave to ferment in a warm place for 15 minutes.

Add half of the flour, stir, cover and let rise in a warm place for 2-3 hours until double in size.

Now stir in the remaining ingredients. Knead the dough by hand for at least 15 minutes until it is soft and elastic. It should not stick. Cover again, let rise in a warm place until double in size.

for both:

- In the meantime, stir 30 g of flour and 150 ml of cold water into a "cream" and cook it on a low heat until it has thickened a little. Remove from the stove and allow to cool.

Divide the dough into two parts and form each into a flat, almost oval loaf (if necessary, dip your hands in olive oil). Now use a brush to spread the flour cream on top and let rest for 20 minutes.

Preheat the oven and baking tray to 250°. Place a fireproof bowl of hot water on the floor of the oven to prevent the bread from drying out. Bake the baking tray with the bread on the 2nd rack from the bottom for about 8 minutes. Then move the tray to the middle rack. Continue baking until the bread has turned a light brown color.

Jingalov hats – herb-filled flatbread

The spelling varies, and you can also find Zhingyalovs khats and similar compositions on the internet. The name "Jingalov hats" is derived from the Armenian words "jingal" (herbs) and "hats" (bread), which aptly describes the nature of this bread. They are often filled only with herbs and green cabbage or lettuce plants. However, there may be a selection of 10 to 20 different types of these. In this case, less of the bitter, sour and hearty ones are used, and more of the "more neutral-tasting" ones, so that a well-balanced, tasty filling is created.

The ingredients used include parsley, dill, coriander, spinach, kale, lettuce, beet tops, Swiss chard, chickweed, shepherd's purse, young garlic, mint, basil, sorrel, cress, burnet, borage, chervil, chives and many more.

Ingredients for 8-10 pieces
500 g flour
400-450 ml lukewarm water
1 tsp salt
a little oil if necessary

Filling
a large bowl herbs and greens to taste, finely chopped
olive oil, salt, pepper
optional: grated goat's cheese, fried onions
Butter or oil for frying

- Mix the flour and water to form a smooth dough, adding more flour or water if necessary. Cover and leave to rest for 30 minutes.

- In the meantime, wash and dry the herbs, chop them finely and mix them well in a large bowl. Season generously with 1 tablespoon of olive oil, salt and pepper, knead well and mix.

- Divide the dough into 8 to 10 balls. Roll out each ball into a thin ellipse.

- • Place as much of the herb filling as possible (2-3 tablespoons) on the dough ellipse, fold the dough and close the opening like a seam over the herbs (press together and, if necessary, turn over). Now carefully beat the filled dough by hand as flat as the filling allows.

- Bake in a non-stick pan for 3-4 minutes on each side.

- Tip: blend the already chopped herb mixture in a blender together with oil, salt and pepper to create a kind of herb paste. This makes it easier to measure out and use for filling the bread.
See foto on next page.

Jingalov hats

Georgia

Khachapuri – Georgian cheese bread

Stuffed cheese flatbreads are the quintessential Georgian dish. Every region, indeed every family, has its own variation. Of the 14 official Georgian cheeses made from buffalo, cow, goat, or sheep milk, the brined cheese sulguni is the most popular.

In principle, you can use any cheese you like. It is also common to mix two types of cheese together. In Europe, you can use a ⅔ to ⅓ mixture of grated mozzarella with sheep's cheese or another hearty cheese such as Parmigiano, Gorgonzola, Camembert/Brie, or Pecorino.

They can be baked in the form of a filled round flatbread or shaped into a small "ship". This tradition comes from Adjara on the Black Sea. An egg is often cracked into the "ships"; this symbolizes the sun, which the sailors use to navigate. These cheese sandwiches are also popular in Russia. The boats are called "lodka" in Russian or khachapuri adjaruli in Georgia.

The breads turn out best if you leave the dough to rise in the fridge for 24 hours.

Plan 1 day ahead if necessary.

Ingredients for the dough for 8 loaves

1 kg fine wheat or spelt flour

1 sachet of yeast (or 100 g sourdough and ½ sachet of yeast, then use 100 g less flour)

2 tsp salt

1 teaspoon sugar

250 g lukewarm water

120 g oil

Ingredients for the cheese filling as desired, e.g.

600 g mozzarella

200 g sheep's cheese from the brine

100 g pecorino

1 egg

some flour

For sprinkling/topping:

optional 1 tbsp milk, 8 eggs, 20 g butter, grated cheese, herbs (chives, parsley, coriander, chopped spring onions)

- Mix the dough ingredients and knead well to form an elastic dough. Shape into a ball and oil. Cover and leave to rise in the fridge for 12 hours. Knead again, shape back into a ball, oil and leave to rise again in the fridge for another 12 hours. Now divide into 6 portioned balls and leave to reach room temperature on a baking tray.

- In the meantime, grate the cheese and mix with 1 egg and a little flour.

- Preheat the oven and baking tray to 230°. Place a bowl of hot water on the bottom of the oven.

Variant 1/ flatbread:

- Instead of several portioned flatbreads, you can also bake 1 large cheese loaf in a springform pan using the same principle.

- If you opt for several small flatbreads, roll out the portion balls into small circles on baking paper.

- Shape the cheese mixture into a ball and place in the center of the circle. Close the circle of dough over the ball and swirl well.

- Place it with the "seal" side down and carefully roll it flat.

- Prick a few holes with a fork. Brush with egg yolk.

- Using the baking paper, carefully slide onto the hot baking tray and reduce the temperature to 200°. Bake for approx. 25 minutes until golden brown. Serve lukewarm.

Variant 2/ boats:

- Roll out the balls into circles on baking paper. Roll up from two sides to the middle and twist the ends. Then carefully roll the rolls outwards again until the pastry is roughly the shape of a boat. See drawing.
- Put some cheese mixture in the middle. Brush the edges with egg

yolk and sprinkle with cheese if necessary. Using the baking paper, carefully slide onto the hot baking tray and lower the temperature to approx. 200°.

- Bake for 15 minutes until the pastry starts to turn light brown. Now take it out, make a small dent with a spoon and crack an egg into it. Bake for a further 10 minutes until the egg white has set. Remove, leave to cool slightly and serve lukewarm.

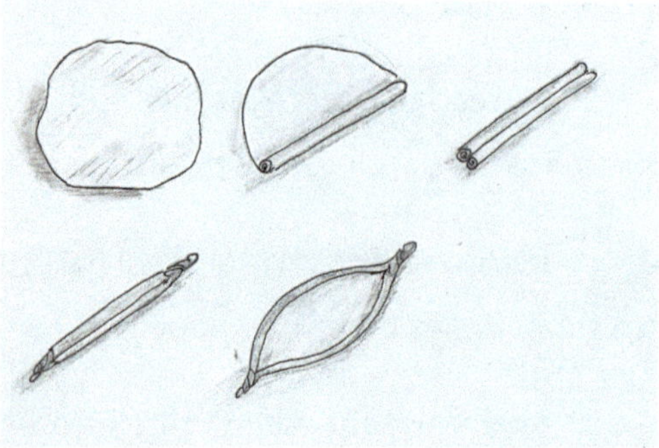

- Spread butter flakes on the boat.
- To eat: break off some of the edge and dip into the egg yolk

Mtschadi –Cornbread patties

Quick rolls from the pan, a specialty from western Georgia.

Ingredients for approx. 12 small rolls
500 g corn flour
approx. 400 g hot water
1 tsp salt
or
200 ml whole milk, 100 ml hot water
300 g fine corn semolina (instant polenta)
3 tbsp vegetable oil
sea salt
oil for frying

- Mix the salt and flour, gradually add the hot water and hot milk. Bring to the boil briefly if necessary. The dough will not feel like wheat flour, but more like wet sand. Leave to soak for 20 minutes and knead.
- Shape about 10-12 small balls with wet hands and form 0.7 to 1 cm thick, small flat cakes about 8 cm in diameter.
- Add oil to the pan and fry on both sides until golden brown. Serve warm.

Variante:

Chvishtari, Maisbrot mit Käse aus Swanetien:

- In a bowl, mix 100 g hot whole milk and 200 g hot water with 160 g instant corn semolina, add salt. Mix in an egg. Add 150 g hard cheese and 150 g grated brine cheese to the batter.

Mtschadi

Tschudu – filled flatbread

from Dagestan / North Caucasus

You can travel through the seasons with chudu: In spring it is filled with herbs and spring onions, in autumn with pumpkin and caramelized onions. Minced meat is just as popular as tvorog, the Russian cottage cheese. In Germany, you can find it in Russian supermarkets. Instead of tworog for the filling, other cream cheeses such as German cottage cheese, ricotta or brine cheese are also suitable. If you have time, you can easily make it yourself from fresh milk.

Ingredients for approx. 8 pieces

500 g flour
300 ml kefir
1 egg
30 ml oil
½ tsp salt
½ tsp baking powder
Butter for spreading
Oil or butter for frying

Ingredients for the filling

250 g Russian cottage cheese Tworog
150 g spicy grated cheese
40 g parsley
salt, pepper
Parsley or mixed herbs

- Knead the dough ingredients into a smooth dough, shape into a ball and rub with olive oil. Cover with cling film and leave to rest for 30 minutes.

- Form approx. 8 balls and roll out into flat circles. Cover one side, fold over and press the edges firmly. Heat the oil, butter or a mixture of both in a non-stick frying pan and bake the loaves on both sides. Once baked, brush one side with butter and serve warm.

Tschudu

Azerbaijan

Azerbaijani cuisine is influenced by Turkey (such as dolma or kebab), Armenia and Iran (milk bread, allash, meat with nuts and sour fruit) and Central Asia (plov). Azerbaijan also offers a wide selection of breads, including yukha, yayma, fatir, fasali, kata and tandir. In addition to the clay oven bread tandir, the well-known lavash (see Iran) and the sweet milk bread chorek are among the most popular. The delicious qutab always goes down a treat!

Qutab – stuffed flatbread

Ingredients for 4 pieces
250 g flour
1 teaspoon salt
2 tablespoons olive oil
150 ml lukewarm water

For the filling
4 spring onions, finely chopped
4 sprigs of dill
4 sprigs of flat-leaf parsley
200 g hard cheese or brined cheese to taste, grated

- Knead the dough ingredients into a smooth dough, shape into a ball, and rub with olive oil. Cover (preferably with plastic wrap) and let rest for 30 minutes.

- In the meantime, prepare the filling: chop the herbs, grate the cheese, and mix everything with the chopped onions.

- Divide the dough into four parts and form into balls. Roll these out into thin circles and top each with a quarter of the filling. Fold over, press the edges firmly, and bake on both sides on a baking sheet or in a nonstick pan without fat.

Qutab

Chorek – Sweet milk bread

Sweet bread, which is also found in Iran and is called sherma there, is baked on Nowruz Day, the Persian New Year, which coincides with the beginning of spring on the equinox and on other holidays.

Milk bread with a sweet spread is ideal for breakfast or afternoon tea, but it can also be eaten with (fresh) cheese or chickpea purée.

The spice mahlab is made from dried cherry pits and has a slightly bitter almond flavor. It can be found in Turkish stores or online.

Tip: Instead of small rolls, you can also bake a braided yeast plait from the dough.

Ingredients for four milk breads
500 g flour
120 ml lukewarm water
120 ml lukewarm milk
2 tsp sugar
2 tsp powdered sugar
1 tsp dry yeast
1 egg yolk for the dough
½ tsp cardamom, ginger, or cinnamon, or 1 tbsp mahlab
120 ml neutral oil
¼ tsp saffron
1 egg yolk for brushing, 1 tablespoon boiling water, white sesame seeds

- Mix the yeast, sugar, and lukewarm water to form a pre-dough and let it ferment for 15 minutes.
- Grind the saffron in a mortar and pour 1 tablespoon of boiling water over it, then let it steep for 10 minutes. Preheat the oven to 220°C.
- Beat 1 egg yolk with powdered sugar, then add lukewarm milk, spices, salt, and oil. Add to the pre-dough. Stir in flour.
- Cover the resulting dough and let it rest for 45 minutes. Divide into 4 parts, form balls, and flatten them (1-2 cm). Place on a baking sheet lined with parchment paper.
- Mix the saffron water with the second egg yolk, brush the dough pieces with it, and sprinkle with sesame seeds.
- Place a small bowl of boiling water in the oven.
- Place the baking sheet with the bread in the oven and bake for about 20-30 minutes, depending on the oven.

Iran

The word "naan," meaning "bread," originates from Persian and later spread to India, Pakistan, Afghanistan, and Azerbaijan. Among Turkic peoples, it is called "nan" or "non."

Naan-e-barbari

This Iranian-Afghan flatbread is oval in shape and is originally 60-80 cm long. For a standard household oven, it inevitably has to be made smaller. No one knows exactly where the name "barbari" comes from. One theory is that it was brought over by Hazara immigrants from Afghanistan, as they are known there as talented bakers.

Traditionally, the bread is baked in a tannour/tandoor, hence the name naan-e-tandoori or naan-e-tabrizi, bread from Tabriz. It works just as well in an electric oven, but you have to do without the smoky flavor.

The dough should rest for up to 12 hours, preferably overnight in the refrigerator. This means you need less yeast, the yeast flavor is reduced, and the bread stays fresh longer. If you're in a hurry, use more yeast and let the dough rise for 1 hour in a warm place.

Ingredients for two loaves:

900 g wheat flour

650 ml lukewarm water

15 g dry yeast (1.5 packets) or 1 cube fresh yeast

1 tbsp sugar

1 heaped tsp salt

4 tbsp olive oil

For brushing and sprinkling:

3 tablespoons olive oil or butter

Milk

Water

Sesame seeds

Black cumin seeds

- Knead a smooth dough, rub with oil, cover, and let rise in a warm place for 1 hour. Or prepare with half the yeast and cover with plastic wrap and refrigerate overnight. Halve the dough and knead each half again on a floured surface.
- Flatten the first half into an oval shape and place on a baking sheet lined with parchment paper. Brush the dough with a little milk. Use your fingertips to press the typical longitudinal grooves into the flatbread. Sprinkle with sesame seeds and black cumin. Prick the grooves with a fork. Let the bread rest for 30 minutes.
- Preheat the oven to 220°C.
- Press down the grooves again with your fingertips, then place

the bread directly into the oven and bake for approx. 15 minutes.

- In the meantime, prepare the second loaf of bread.

- Remove the finished bread from the oven and (optionally) sprinkle it immediately with a little water and brush with a little olive oil or melted butter. Cover with a kitchen towel for a few minutes and allow the fat to soak in.

Naan-e-barbari

Naan-e-lavash

The wafer-thin lavash flatbreads (lavash means "delicate, thin") are made without yeast, using only flour, salt, and water. This bread can also be found in Armenia, Azerbaijan, Georgia, Kurdistan, and Turkey.

When yeast is added, it becomes naan-e-taftoon.

In commercial bakeries, lavash flatbreads measuring 60-80 cm are baked in traditional tanour ovens.

Ingredients for 8 flatbreads:
300 g flour
1 tsp salt
200 ml lukewarm water

- Knead the dough for 10 minutes and leave to rest, covered, for 30 minutes.
- Roll into approx. 8 balls, dust with flour and cover. Roll out each ball as thinly as possible with a rolling pin. Bake in a large pan or on a baking sheet for approx. ½ minute, turning repeatedly until the flatbread forms large bubbles.
- Stack on a plate and cover with a cloth to prevent them from drying out. Once all the flatbreads are baked, place the covered plate in a plastic bag.
- If you want to use the flatbreads as wraps, do so immediately

while they are still warm.

- When they become cold and hard, they can be used like crackers, for example in a Syrian bread salad called "fattoush."

Naan-e-lavash

Naan-e-taftoon

In Iran, there are traditionally four types of bread, each with its own bakery. Taftoon, which used to be made from barley flour, is a crispy, cracker-like bread that is baked by sticking it to the hot wall of a clay oven, as the word suggests. Taftan also means "something that is grilled/baked under the hot sun."

450 g flour
250 g yogurt/buttermilk/quark/kefir
1 packet yeast, 1 teaspoon salt
20-50 ml lukewarm water

- Make a smooth dough from the ingredients and knead for 10 minutes. Form a ball, brush with oil, cover, and let rise in an oiled bowl in a warm place for 1 hour. Then "degas" the dough by pressing it flat from the inside out and let it rest for another 30 minutes.

- Flatten with your hands and fingertips until it is about the thickness of a thick pancake; the flatbread is thinner than naan-e-barbari but thicker than lavash. Work it again with your fingertips so that dents and tiny holes appear all over it. Bake on both sides in a hot, coated pan or on a baking sheet; this takes about 5 minutes per bread.

- Taftoon tastes best warm from the pan.

Naan - e- Taftoon

Naan-e-sangak

A whole grain bread for ambitious hobby bakers!

Naan-e-sangak is traditionally baked on a bed of hot stones. The word "sang" means "small stone" or "pebble" in Farsi. Naan-e-sangak was the bread of the Persian army during the reign of Shah Abbas in the 16th century. To ensure that there was enough bread for all the soldiers, each soldier carried a small bag of pebbles with him, which were collected in the evening at the camp and used as a base for baking. Sangak bakeries are so famous that there is even a popular pantomime entertainment dance about them. The Persian baker's dance "Shaateri" (from Shaater = baker) is a Ravajati dance, i.e., a narrative dance, and is set in just such a sangak bakery.

Baking sangak bread at home is quite an adventurous undertaking and will most likely not turn out perfectly the first time. To convert a standard electric stove into a "sangak oven," you need clean river pebbles and a sturdy baking sheet with high sides. The stones should be as smooth as possible and, above all, small, as they will not stick so firmly to the bread and will not tear holes in the surface when removed. I only had coarse decorative gravel available and therefore had exactly this problem. Original sangak stones are hardly bigger than broad beans (fava beans). Since wood-fired ovens get much hotter than a typical home oven, a pizza stone under the baking tray or a hot air (instead of convection) oven will give even better results.

If you have ready-made sourdough to hand, you can get started right away. Otherwise, plan ahead and make your own pre-ferment first.

You can use sourdough starter instead of commercial yeast to obtain a more aromatic wild yeast dough.

In any case – whether you use sourdough starter or commercial yeast – the dough needs plenty of time to rest, rise, and develop its flavor.

Start 2 days in advance!

Ingredients
For the pre-dough
½ cup whole wheat flour
½ cup wheat flour (type 550)
Water
Salt, ½ teaspoon dry yeast
1 teaspoon sugar

Mix a soft, almost mushy dough, cover with cling film, and place in the refrigerator overnight.

For the bread dough
200 g whole wheat flour
200 g wheat flour
½ teaspoon salt
2 glasses of water
½ teaspoon baking soda
For sprinkling (optional) Sesame seeds, poppy seeds

- In a medium-sized bowl, mix the flour, pre-dough, and 1½ cups of warm water. Stir with a spatula or fork until a wet, sticky dough forms.
- Cover and let rest at room temperature for 2 hours.
- Knead the dough with a scooping and folding motion, cover, and let rest for 30 minutes.

- Repeat the kneading process and let rest for another 30 minutes.

Place in the refrigerator and let rest overnight.

- The next day, divide the dough into 4 equal pieces and let come to room temperature while you preheat the oven. If you have a pizza stone, place it on the lowest rack of the oven.

- Line the baking sheet (with high sides) with clean stones and place it on the pizza stone.

- Preheat the oven to the highest temperature, if possible to 260°-300° degrees.

- In the meantime, shape the bread. Moisten the work surface and your hands with water to prevent sticking.

- Carefully place one of the pieces of dough on the wet work surface and stretch it with your hands until you have a large, thin oval or triangle, slightly smaller than the baking tray. The dough is very soft.

- Carefully remove the hot baking tray with the stones from the oven and carefully slide the shaped bread onto the stones.

- Sprinkle the bread with sesame or poppy seeds as desired and carefully return the tray to the lowest rack of the oven.

- Bake until golden brown, about 8 minutes at the specified temperature. If necessary, bake a little longer. If the oven bakes unevenly, turn the tray over once (front edge to the back). When the bread is baked to the point that it comes away from the base, turn it over. Small stones may still be stuck to the surface. Bake for a few more minutes until golden brown all over.

- Remove from the oven and use ice cube tongs to remove the stones from the bread, if necessary.

- Caution: If the bread remains in the oven for too long, the stones will bake into the bread, especially if they are not flat, and it will be impossible to remove them without destroying the entire surface.

(Foto'Wikipedia)

Original-Sangak

my own attempt, but the stones were too big

above - own attempt

Uzbekistan

Uzbek-Kyrgyz "Lepyoschka" (Tandyr Naan, Patyr Naan), known as "Lepeschka" in Uzbek, is a round white bread baked in a tandyr, the well-known clay oven. A meal without Lepeschka is not a complete meal in Uzbekistan. Traditionally, the bread is never cut with a knife, as this is considered rude, but is always broken into pieces by hand. Breaking bread together seals engagements and contracts, and when someone goes away for a long time, they must bite off a small piece of a fresh loaf, while the rest of the loaf is kept until their return.

Lepeshkas are already served for breakfast, together with juicy melons and sweet grapes, and they are obligatory for lunch and dinner: they are always bought in even numbers.

Lepeshka – Uzbek flatbread –

The bread is round in shape with a patterned "center" that remains thin and crispy when baked, in contrast to the thicker, soft crust. Every Uzbek city has its own style and specialties. There are homemade flatbreads (obi non), meat-filled, baked with bran, fried with onions in oil, or made from "puff pastry."

In Uzbekistan, there are special walnut wood tools for rolling out and shaping the dough. Once the bread has been shaped, the flatbreads are stamped. There is a wide range of motifs to choose from: mostly flowers, but sometimes also the baker's phone number.

With a little luck, you can find Uzbek bread stamps and rolling devices for sale on Etsy or eBay. In Uzbekistan and many other countries in Central Asia, bread was often stamped with special stamps or patterns to identify and distinguish it when it was baked in the communal village oven, as not every household had its own oven. The stamps served to identify the owner, decorate the bread, ensure consistency and uniformity, and, last but not least, were religious or symbolic patterns intended to bring good luck and blessings. The stamped golden-brown bread certainly looks very pretty, and even today you won't find bread without stamp decorations in Uzbekistan.

Like all bread, before the invention of instant yeast, it was made with sourdough (Hamir-Truch or Hamir-My).

A mixture of sourdough and yeast is guaranteed to work. If you want the dough to be sweet, add 1-2 tablespoons of sweetened condensed milk.

Ingredients for sourdough bread

- 320 g flour
- 140 g sourdough
- 60 ml lukewarm water
- 1/2 tsp dry yeast
- 1 tsp sugar
- 1 heaped tsp salt
- 1 tbsp melted butter

Ingredients for yeast bread

- 400 g flour
- 220 ml lukewarm water
- 1 packet dry yeast
- 1 teaspoon sugar
- 1 heaped teaspoon salt
- 1 tablespoon melted butter

For brushing: either water, milk, egg yolk mixed with 2 tablespoons of milk, or water mixed with a little crème fraîche.

- Knead a smooth dough and shape into one or two balls. Brush with oil or leave to rise under a damp cloth for 2-3 hours. Now roll out the flatbreads so that they are flat on the inside and have a thick, bulging edge on the outside. But they can also be rolled out into large circular flatbreads.

- If you have stamps, you can stamp them now. Don't be hesitant, but press the stamp firmly into the dough, otherwise the patterns will no longer be visible after baking.

- Preheat the oven to 240°C convection and preheat the baking sheet

- Brush the flatbreads with water, milk, egg milk, or watery crème fraîche. Bake for about 15-20 minutes until golden brown, depending on your oven.

- The results are even better with a convection oven, which reduces the baking time to 10-12 minutes and the temperature to 220°C.

Katlama – puff pastry flatbread

This delicious filled puff pastry flatbread can be folded in different ways. Either in a similar way to Moroccan msemen, but filled, or in a circular layer as shown in the photo. It can be filled with lard (from lamb) without any other ingredients, with lard and finely chopped, braised onions, with spicy minced meat, or with butter, spring onions, spinach, dill, and brined cheese. It is important that the dough is rolled out very thinly.

Ingredients for 6 flatbreads
600 g flour
350 ml lukewarm water
1 tbsp oil
1 tsp salt

Spring onion and cheese filling
1 bunch of spring onions, finely chopped
300 g brined cheese, crumbled
1 bunch of dill or 2 handfuls of spinach leaves, finely chopped
Salt, nutmeg
200 g butter, melted-

- Mix the filling ingredients (except for the butter) until crumbly and chill.
- Knead a smooth dough, adding water or flour as needed. Cover and let rest for 20 minutes.
- For the layered circle, divide the dough into six balls.

- Roll out each ball very thinly with a little flour. Place a pot lid in the middle and cut eight times around the lid to the edge.

- Brush the middle thinly with melted butter/lard. Spread a little of the filling on top.

- Pull the first of the eight dough sections from the edge and along the edge over the entire round middle.

- Spread with butter/lard again and add a little filling.

- Continue until you have a compact round flatbread.

- Fry on both sides for approx. 10 minutes in a buttered/oiled pan over medium heat.

- Cover with a lid to ensure that it cooks through on the inside. Enjoy lukewarm or cold.

Afghanistan

Afghanistan is surrounded by numerous countries, including Pakistan, China, and Uzbekistan. Accordingly, it has also absorbed influences in its cuisine.

Naan bread – flatbread

Ingredients for 2 loaves:
280 g wheat flour
60 g whole wheat flour
1.5 tsp dry yeast
1 tsp salt
80 g melted butter
120 ml lukewarm water

For the glaze
1 tbsp wheat flour
80 ml water

For sprinkling: sesame seeds and black cumin seeds (nigella sativa)

- Knead the dough ingredients into an elastic dough and leave to rise, covered, in a warm place for at least 1 hour.

- Dust the work surface with flour. Halve the dough and roll out each piece thinly (approx. 0.5 cm) into an oval shape.

- To brush, mix 1 tbsp flour with 4 tbsp water (approx. 80 ml). Brush both flatbreads thinly with the flour-water mixture and use your fingers to press even, deep, parallel lines lengthwise into both breads. Sprinkle the breads with a little sesame seeds and black cumin.

- Let rest for another 15 minutes, then press down the grooves again so that they do not disappear during baking. Preheat the oven to 180°-200°.

- Place both flatbreads side by side on a baking sheet lined with parchment paper. Bake in the preheated oven for approx. 15 minutes. The baking time varies depending on the oven.

Tip: Instead of whole wheat flour, bake with a little rye flour!

Bolani – Stuffed flatbread

In Afghanistan, bolani is a popular street food sold by vendors in markets and alleyways. It is also a staple of family meals and celebrations. Filled with potatoes, green onions, and fresh cilantro, and seasoned with turmeric and cumin, this bread is a delicious, filling snack, a "bread time" in the truest sense of the word. Other popular fillings include pumpkin or leek. It goes well with refreshing yogurt sauces with cucumber and mint or with tomatoes and onions.

Ingredients for 8 flatbreads:
400 g flour
175 ml water
1 tsp salt
5 tsp oil

Filling
4 medium potatoes, boiled and mashed
1.5 bunches of spring onions, finely chopped
1 bunch of coriander, finely chopped
Pepper, salt
Served with a sauce made from 300 g plain yogurt
1 clove of garlic, pressed
1 tsp fresh or dried dill
0.5 tsp ground coriander
Salt
Oil or butter for frying

- Knead a smooth dough, form a ball, rub with oil, and wrap in plastic wrap. Let rest for 30 minutes.
- Mix herbs and mashed potatoes, season.
- Prepare the yogurt sauce.
- Divide the dough into 8 balls. Roll out each ball very thinly, spread with 2 tablespoons of filling, fold over and press down the edges firmly so that they do not open.
- Fry in a non-stick pan in good oil or butter until brown on both sides. Serve warm.

Sweet bread – Root

Lightly crispy on the outside and soft on the inside, the special ingredients give Afghan bread root its distinctive taste and make it a popular delicacy in Afghan cuisine. A cross between a biscuit and a cake, it goes well with black and green tea or coffee. It can also be served with jam and cream.

Ingredients for 1 baking sheet:

300 g flour
150 g whole grain spelt flour
3 tsp baking powder
100 g ground almonds
120-150 g brown sugar
1 tsp ground cardamom
1/2 tsp ground saffron
1 egg
1 pinch of salt
120 ml milk or yogurt
60 ml neutral oil or clarified butter/ghee

Brush with: 1 egg yolk, 1 tbsp milk
Sprinkle with: ½ cup sesame seeds, ½ cup black cumin seeds

• Dissolve the saffron in hot water. Knead together the wheat flour, whole spelt flour, baking powder, ground almonds, brown sugar, cardamom, saffron, egg, oil, and salt. Then gradually add the milk until a firm, even dough is formed. Wrap the dough in plastic wrap and let it rest for 30 minutes.

- Preheat the oven to 225°C, line a baking sheet with parchment paper, and mix the black cumin and sesame seeds. Beat the egg yolk with the milk in a small bowl.

- Remove the dough from the plastic wrap and roll out to a thickness of about ½ cm. Carefully place on the parchment paper and baking sheet: you may want to roll it out directly on the parchment paper. Now prick the dough several times with a fork. You can also use this to create a pattern of your choice.

- Brush the dough with the milk and egg yolk mixture, sprinkle generously with black cumin and sesame seeds, and place on the middle rack of the oven. Bake at 225°C for about 20 minutes until the surface is golden brown.

- Remove, allow to cool, and cut into squares, diamonds, or triangles.

India

The list of Indian flatbreads is long. Filled or unfilled, baked or fried, made from different flours, seasoned or unseasoned. They are all served fresh and accompany dhals and curries, chutneys and raitas.

The well-known naan is available plain, with herbs, or spread with ghee. Parathas come in various varieties and are folded flatbreads, similar to Tunisian and Moroccan mlaoui. Chapati or roti are simple flatbreads that can be made from various flours or flour mixtures. Puri are small fried dough balls that are also sold filled as street food. Bathura are the big sisters of puri, also fried balls, but made from a different dough. Finally, papadam are cracker-like crispy flatbreads made from legume flours such as chickpeas or lentils, comparable to Mexican tacos. If you like to try new things, you have a wide selection here.

Naan – flatbread

The use of yogurt and milk makes this flatbread very tasty and fluffy.

Ingredients for 10 small flatbreads:

500 g wheat flour

150 g yogurt (Greek thick yogurt with 10% fat works well)

150 g milk

150 g milk

1 egg

1 packet dry yeast

1 teaspoon sugar

1 teaspoon salt

2 tablespoons olive oil or melted butter for the dough

Melted butter or olive oil for brushing after baking

Optional: 2 cloves garlic, crushed, for the melted butter for brushing

- First mix the dry ingredients, then stir in the remaining ingredients. Add flour if the dough is too thin, or milk if it is too thick.
- Knead for 10 minutes. Cover and leave to rest in a warm place for 1 hour.
- Form 10 balls, roll out to a thickness of 1 cm and bake on both sides without fat, preferably in a cast iron pan.
- After baking, brush with (garlic) butter or oil if desired.

Naan flatbread

Chapati or roti –

flatbread made from flour mixtures

Chapati, also known as roti, is a traditional Indian flatbread. It is often made from wheat flour, water, and salt. The bread is baked on a hot tawa pan or in a tandoor oven.

Chapatis are thin, round, and slightly elastic, which makes them easy to fold or roll.

In addition to chapatis made from wheat flour, there are also varieties made from other types of flour.

Bajra chapati: Bajra, also known as pearl millet, is a commonly used flour in the western regions of India. Bajra chapatis have a strong flavor and are rich in fiber.

Makki Roti: These are chapatis made from corn flour. They are particularly popular in the northern regions of India and have a slightly crumbly texture.

Jowar Roti: Jowar, also known as sorghum, is a gluten-free grain from the sweet grass family, also known as black millet or sugar millet. Jowar rotis are common in many parts of India and have a slight sweetness and a softer consistency.

Nachni Roti: Nachni, also known as finger millet or amaranth, is processed into a nutrient-rich flour. Nachni rotis are dark in color and have a slightly earthy flavor.

These different types of flour give the chapatis a unique taste and texture. They are often associated with regional cuisines and are used according to preference and availability of ingredients. One variation is the so-called phulka, which are roasted over an open flame and puff up like small puri flatbreads.

Zutaten für 16 Fladen
400g Chapati Mehl oder weißes Weizenmehl
1 TL Salz
240 ml Wasser
10 EL flüssiges Ghee oder Butter

- Put the flour in a bowl, add salt, and gradually stir in the water with a whisk, stirring constantly. As soon as the dough begins to thicken, continue kneading by hand. Add a little more water if necessary. Knead thoroughly on the work surface until a soft and smooth dough forms after a few minutes.

- Now shape into a ball, brush with a little liquid ghee/butter and leave to rest for 20-30 minutes, covered with a damp towel.

- Divide the dough ball into 16 pieces and roll them out on a floured work surface into flat, circular flatbreads about 15 cm in diameter.

- Fold the damp towel into a square and keep it ready next to the stove. Heat a coated cast iron pan without fat. Place a flatbread in the pan and brown lightly for 10-20 seconds. Turn and brown on the other side.

- Now turn the flatbread again. If it is bubbling, press down lightly with the towel. Fry until brown spots appear on the surface. Remove and either serve immediately or brush with liquid ghee, cover, and keep fresh until serving.

Chapati

Puri – small balloon flatbreads

They are a delicious, light, almost chip-like side dish that accompanies many Asian dishes. In India, they are also filled and served with a special sauce as street food.

Ingredients for approx. 20 pieces (2 people)
150 g chapati flour or white wheat flour (type 405)
Salt
8 tablespoons lukewarm water
Oil for your hands
Flour for rolling out
1 liter frying oil (canola oil, corn oil, or peanut oil)

- Knead the flour with salt and warm water thoroughly to form a firm dough. Wrap the dough in plastic wrap and let it rest for 30 minutes.

- Roll out the dough on a floured surface to a thickness of about 1 mm. Cut out dough discs approx. 5 cm in diameter using a cookie cutter (a glass will also work). If they are larger, they will not form balls, but will instead look more like small bathura bread, which of course does not detract from the taste.

- Heat the oil in a pot. When bubbles rise around a wooden stick held in the oil, it is ready for frying.

- Use a slotted spoon to slide the dough discs into the oil and press them down gently until they puff up. This happens quite quickly. Then remove the spoon and let them brown a little more while floating on top.

- Remove the crispy balls and drain on paper towels. They are usually served hot, but they stay crispy for a day in dry air.

Bathura – Balloon bread

Voluminous and airy: Bathura is made from a special dough that rises into a large and airy bread. It is crispy on the outside and pleasantly soft on the inside. This combination of textures makes it a unique culinary experience. It is served as the perfect accompaniment to hearty dishes such as lentils, chickpea curry, or potato curry. It absorbs the flavors of the sauces and complements them perfectly.

Bathura is often refined with spices such as cumin, coriander, or garlic, which give the bread an intense flavor.

The most important thing for success is that the dough is rolled out really thinly. If the dough is 2 mm thick, the flatbread remains flat and does not puff up.

The fat should be hot, but not smoking. For the first 5 seconds, the flatbread must be pressed down with a ladle so that it puffs up. Then immediately turn it over and fry the other side.

Ingredients for 6 pieces
200 g flour
35 g fine soft wheat semolina
80 tablespoons yogurt or buttermilk
1 tablespoon olive oil
½ teaspoon baking powder
1 pinch baking soda
1/2 teaspoon salt
1 teaspoon sugar
optional ½ teaspoon cumin / ground coriander

garlic paste

50-60 ml lukewarm water

approx. 2 l frying oil ca. 2 l Frittieröl

- Knead the ingredients into a smooth dough (5 minutes with a machine, 10 minutes by hand) and let it rest for 2-4 hours.
- Roll into 6 small balls and roll out to a thickness of 1 mm.
- Immediately place in 180°C hot frying oil and leave submerged (5-7 seconds), then turn over until a balloon has formed. One bread roll takes no longer than approx. 30 seconds.

Paratha – folded flatbread

Paratha is a thin flatbread that bears a striking resemblance to Moroccan and Tunisian mlaoui flatbreads. The term is composed of para & atta, which means "layers of baked dough."

In India, it is made with ghee, which causes the bread to harden quickly in cool European weather. If you make it with yogurt instead of water, the flatbread stays soft and fresh longer.

Ingredients for 16 small flatbreads
500 g flour
250 ml lukewarm water (optionally, partly yogurt)
1 tsp salt
8 tsp ghee or olive oil

- Knead all ingredients into a relatively firm, yet soft and elastic, non-sticky dough. This takes about 6-8 minutes in a food processor.
- Divide into 16 small balls and rub with oil. Let rest for 30 minutes.
- Roll out the balls into thin circles and brush with ghee/oil, fold one half toward the center, brush, fold the other half over the top, brush, fold one long side toward the center, brush, fold the other long side over the top, turn over. Set aside.
- Tip: You can also dust the coated layers lightly with flour to make the flatbreads even more "flaky."
- Fold all balls into parcels (see page 40).

- Then, in the same order, roll out the parcels into thin, square flatbreads and bake on both sides in a hot (coated) pan or on a baking sheet until light brown spots appear. If necessary, press the edges down slightly. If you bake them only until lukewarm, they will become dry and hard. So you have to work relatively quickly. They taste best when freshly baked.
- Stack the finished flatbreads on a plate, cover with a cloth, and place in a plastic bag to keep them warm and soft for longer.

Basic sourdough recipe

Sourdough is an alternative or additional leavening agent for baking. If cared for properly, it will last "forever" and give bread a stronger flavor. It is ideal for those who do not like the taste of yeast. Sourdough bread is easier to digest than yeast bread and stays fresh longer.

Making your own sourdough is not difficult—all you need is flour and water and the right temperature to produce the starter for sourdough bread and rolls, which can be used again and again. Temperatures between 30° and 35° are ideal. If it is cooler, it takes longer. At temperatures above 45°, the yeast is no longer viable.

Total ingredients
350 g flour – (rye or wheat, depending on the type of bread)
350 ml lukewarm water gesamt

Preparation

Duration: approx. 5 days

Day 1

Mix 100 g flour with 100 ml lukewarm water in a large bowl (beat thoroughly) and leave to rest, covered, for 12 hours.

Stir again and leave to rest for another 12 hours.

Day 2

Add 50 g flour and 50 ml lukewarm water to the dough, beat and cover. Leave to rest for 24 hours. Depending on the outside temperature, fermentation should now slowly begin. The dough should smell sour and yeasty. The sour smell will diminish slightly after a few days.

Day 3

Add 100 g flour and 100 ml lukewarm water. Leave the dough to rest for 12 hours, beat it, then leave it to rest for another 12 hours.

The smell will become more intense and yeasty.

Day 4

Add 100 g flour and 100 ml lukewarm water and beat the dough. Leave the dough to rest for 24 hours.

The dough is now ready to bake. You now have a finished starter, from which you usually remove approx. 100 g and replenish with 50 g each of flour and water. The sourdough can be stored in a wire-clasp jar in the refrigerator for the next baking session. Tip: When using wholemeal flour, more water may be required. This varies depending on the type of flour. Throughout the entire process, the dough should have a pancake-like consistency. The finished sourdough has a pleasant sour smell. If this is not the case and it smells like rotten eggs, the lactic acid bacteria have lost the race and the spoilage bacteria have prevailed. In this case, unfortunately, it must be discarded.

Baking with sourdough:

The total amount of flour determines how much starter you need for souring. For most breads, this is about 5-10 percent of the total amount of flour.

Storage:

You can store the sourdough in the refrigerator and replenish what you have taken out. The air should be able to escape. So use a glass or plastic container with a cloth cover or a swing top without a rubber insert. If you don't use it for more than 2 weeks, you still have to feed it: remove 1 tablespoonful. Mix 50 g of flour and 50 ml of lukewarm water, leave to stand in a warm place for a few hours and then stir into the sourdough. The sourdough can also be maintained in the refrigerator with sourdough powder mixed 1:1 with water. mit Sauerteig:

If you enjoyed the book, I would appreciate a friendly review on Amazon. (Unfortunately, we self-publishers have no influence on the paper and print quality!)
If you have any questions or suggestions for improvement, please feel free to contact me at: havva@havva.de.
You can find another 700 recipes from around the world on my food blog www.1001food.de. There you will also find stories about life in Tunisia under "Tunesien life." **www.1001food.de.**

www.havva.de's publications to date include:

- Flatbread Expedition: From Marrakesh to Mumbai, 50 Irresistible Recipes (Amazon KdP), german and french edition

- The Tunisia Cookbook, Volume 1 (Drinks, Starters, Soups & Egg Dishes), 2022, german edition

- The Tunisia Cookbook, Volume 2, (Couscous, Makruna, Marga & Fish), Bod 2022, german edition

- The Tunisia Cookbook, Volume 3, (Breads, Cakes & Desserts), Bod 2022, german edition

- Egyptian Cooking – Dishes and Their History, Werkstatt Verlag, 2011 (german edition)

- Orientalischer Tanz - Handbuch für die Tänzerin und Tanzpädagogin, 385 pages, 400 fotos, Verlag Oriental Dance Art 2024, german edition

- Oriental Dance – Raqs Sharqi – Belly Dance (2002),

Imprint ebook: Eva Seyberth, Ain Soltan, Ramada, Lala el Qsar, 2121 Gafsa, Tunisia

About the book

Welcome to a culinary journey in a class of its own!

Do you also have beautiful images of crispy breads and delicious exotic holiday specialties in your mind and want to relive some of your travel memories?

On the “Flatbread Expedition from Marrakesh to Mumbai,” you will discover 50 irresistible recipes in over 80 illustrations from the mysterious bakeries of the Oriental-Asian region. Bring a piece of that vacation feeling to your party or family celebration at home! From hearty Moroccan khobz to delicious parathas from India, this book leaves nothing to be desired. Explore the traditions and secrets of flatbread artistry while sending your senses on an unforgettable taste journey. The “Flatbread Expedition” is a feast for connoisseurs who want to take their cooking skills to a new level. Ready for takeoff? Bon Appétit!

About the author

Eva Seyberth is a trained sculptor, full-time dancer, and passionate amateur chef. Familiar with Oriental culture for many years, the Munich native has traveled throughout North Africa and the countries of the Silk Road and has been living in central Tunisia for several years. She has published several reference books and cookbooks.

Printed in Poland
by Amazon Fulfillment
Poland Sp. z o.o., Wrocław

55409139R00083